RECLAIMING
YOUR
FOCUS

How to Overcome Lost Focus and Pay Attention Again

By

Rosemary Mendoza

COPYRIGHT

Copyright © (Rosemary Mendoza) 2023. All rights reserved

DISCLAIMER

This book is only intended to provide knowledge that is relevant to daily life. Every effort has been made to provide accurate, current, trustworthy and comprehensive information. Consult your therapist for guidance and counselling.

CONTENTS

Introduction

Have you ever read the same passage more than once without understanding a word? Or have you ever faced the teacher while sitting in a class, but you were so preoccupied with your thoughts that you missed everything they said? Or did you lose focus during a meeting as you considered the several items still on your to-do list?

If you've ever found yourself in a circumstance where you were physically there but mentally absent, focus is what is lacking.

The cognitive skill of focus is the capacity to direct your attention to a particular task and be completely immersed in it without interruption.

One crucial cognitive skill that aids in task completion is the capacity to focus. It is essential for tasks like working, studying, reading, and listening. There are actions you may do to focus better and be more productive if you have trouble doing so.

Flow is a state of focused concentration in which you are completely absorbed in the job at hand and don't need to actively block out distracting inputs.

These are some illustrations of what focusing may entail:

- working while seated at your desk and avoiding being sidetracked by other people's workplace chats
- attending a lecture without glancing around at the other students or making notes in your notebook
- taking part in a discussion and paying attention to what the other person is saying without daydreaming
- getting the knowledge from a book without having to read it again
- watching a movie or television show without concurrently browsing on your phone
- concentrating on your studies and finishing the chapter you set out to finish without getting sidetracked

- setting a goal and making it your top priority over everything else in your life

Since it allows you to completely participate in a job without having to remove other ideas or activities from your mental space, being able to focus is vital. Being present at the moment entails being attentive. The best mental state for learning and absorbing information is this one.

While being unfocused might be an issue, being overly focused can also be detrimental. It can be harmful to be so intensely focused on something that you develop tunnel vision and lose awareness of anything else.

Fortunately, we can develop our ability to focus and concentrate as well as learn how to control distractions. You can recognize your distractions and get over any concentration issues with perseverance.

To complete duties during the day, focus is essential. You need to pay attention to driving to work and fastening your shoes. And occasionally, personal distractions interfere with our ability to focus at work and vice versa. One of the reasons it's crucial to establish a healthy work-life balance is that it's hard to enjoy your weekend while you're thinking about your workday.

The next time you find yourself unable to focus on anything, consider this. Take into account these seven rationales:
- You attempt multitasking, which is inefficient.
- Your professional life doesn't reflect your ideals.
- Your job isn't interesting or difficult.
- You must feed your body because you are hungry.
- You haven't been getting enough sleep
- Your stress level is high.
- You are concerned about your financial stability.

Chapter 1

The Focused Mind

It is difficult to remain focused. You take a seat and go to work. You begin working on a report that is due tomorrow by opening a new document. Then, your phone lights up. A buddy sent you an SMS. Do you disregard it and keep your attention on the report? Or do you opt to quickly glance at the message?

These and other decisions occur in your brain hundreds of times each day. Your drive to do excellent work and your innate need to be aware of your surroundings are in a continual state of conflict.

Although the idea of attention sometimes seems hazy, the neurology behind it has been extensively investigated. And as a result, it is simpler to comprehend and manage. How do you focus on what is truly important and learn to control your attention so that you can accomplish your goals more quickly?

You must understand the idea of the attentional field to comprehend what a focused mind is. Everything inside of you, such as feelings, ideas, or bodily sensations, together with everything around you, such as what you see and hear, makes up your attentional field. Focus is the capacity to deliberately pay attention to stimuli coming from inside or outside of you.

Two areas of the brain are involved in how you control your attention while you're attempting to focus on something and get a notice. As you begin to concentrate, the prefrontal cortex, which is located right below the brow, becomes active. In the event of a distracting occurrence, the parietal cortex, which is located behind the ear, is stimulated.

Whether working on a tool or constructing a shelter in the distant past, you would have employed your prefrontal cortex. Yet if you had heard a weird noise or been assaulted by a wild animal, your parietal cortex would have immediately been active. As a result, the parietal cortex was first developed as a survival mechanism in the brain to enable us to shift our focus to more important issues in the event of an emergency.

Research demonstrates that the neurons in these two areas release electrical pulses at distinct rates: slower frequencies for the prefrontal region's purposeful and intentional activity, and quicker frequencies for the parietal region's instinctive processing.

Distractions are plentiful and less likely to be essential to our survival in today's society. It gets tougher for us to maintain our attention for extended lengths of time as a result of the constant barrage of conflicting stimuli and information. In other words, it's difficult for us to maintain our concentration.

Keeping The Mind from Wandering

Our brains wander about 50% of the time on average. When we think about things that are not immediately happening around us, reflecting on things that have already happened, could happen in the future, or will never happen at all, we are said to be mind wandering. Studies show that allowing your mind to wander too frequently hurts your general performance in daily life, even though deliberate mind-wandering can be good for your brain—scientists have found that shutting your laptop and daydreaming for a few minutes has a positive impact on cognition. Also, studies demonstrate that excessive mind-wandering has an emotional cost.

Digital distractions like emails or text messages are a big part of what keeps us from doing in-depth work and puts our thoughts on the prowl. While most individuals find it difficult to entirely switch off when working, there are a few strategies to help you focus so you can do more and more quickly.

First, put your phone aside so you can manage your distractions. I mean in another room when I say away. Install some programs that will keep you from using social media on your laptop for a certain period if you are tempted to do so. Yet, controlling your distractions might also include intentionally introducing new ones. According to the Load Theory of Attention, since there are only so many "slots" in your mind, you can run out of space if you try to fill them all. This explains why some individuals focus better when listening to music or having a little background noise.

Watch Your Thoughts: It's difficult to prevent the reality that your thoughts may occasionally stray or that you will be distracted by outside distractions. Focus may be increased by being aware of what your brain is doing. Whenever you find yourself daydreaming, pull your attention back to the activity at hand and indulge yourself when you have a break. It has been demonstrated that this kind of deliberate daydreaming is advantageous for your creativity and productivity. According to other research, telling yourself you'll reward yourself after you finish a task might help you get back on goal after becoming sidetracked. It's not about maintaining constant focus—that would be unrealistic—but rather about keeping track of your attention and employing efficient methods to return it to the work at hand when you become sidetracked.

Develop the neural connections in your brain using a technique that serves as a focused attention exercise for the mind. This exercise, when routinely performed, might make it simpler to maintain your focus in the desired location. Simply bring your attention to your breath, acknowledge that your thoughts have diverted, cut them off, and bring your attention back to your breath. In the long run, the back-and-forth between losing focus and returning to your breath strengthens the brain's circuitry involved in concentration.

Next time you want to maintain your attention on a certain job, try these three strategies. It takes work to cultivate a concentrated mind, and distractions from both internal and external factors will inevitably occur. Recognizing these difficulties will help you handle them more effectively as you develop your mental toughness. Getting into the flow will grow simpler and easier with time and experience.

Chapter 2

Why Can't I Focus

It might be difficult to keep focused for a variety of reasons. Staying focused can be difficult while dealing with things like family issues, a loud environment, work stress, and health issues. The fact is that we are constantly inundated with information and ideas that urge us to let our attention wander. We may not always be incapable of paying attention, then. Simply said, we have a lot of alternatives on what to focus on.

Top Causes of Focus Issues

Personal aspects: Have you slept well enough? Food? Are you maintaining a healthy lifestyle and engaging in exercise? They are all part of the several aspects that might affect our capacity to focus.

Environmental factors: Is a severe blizzard present while you are conducting your quarterly accounting? Maybe you're on the phone as your dog barks at the mailman. Here are a few instances of how the environment might interfere with our ability to think clearly.

Factors affecting the stimulus: You may lose interest in the stimulus if it is uninteresting or lasts for a long period. However, if there are numerous difficult stimuli present, your mind will probably notice and concentrate on the easiest one.

There are several different types of attention problems, including ADD (attention deficit disorder) and ADHD (attention deficit hyperactivity disorder). In fact, according to 2016 research by the CDC, 6.1 million kids in the U.S. have received a diagnosis for one of these illnesses.

If you've ever had a stroke or another type of brain injury, it may have affected your ability to focus. Nevertheless, even in these circumstances, attention may be enhanced over time by adopting healthy daily routines.

Many factors, such as routine behaviors, might impair your capacity to focus. Sometimes, a health problem may be to blame. One of the following health conditions may be indicated by a short attention span:

ADHD. It doesn't simply affect children. The primary signs of this mental health issue in adults include:
- Focusing issues
- Impulsiveness
- Mood changes
- Time management issues.

Anxiety. Focusing might be hampered by worry since worrying requires mental effort. Generalized anxiety disorder symptoms might include:
- Perpetual anxiety
- Fear\sIndecisiveness

Depression. A melancholy mood is only one aspect of this mood disorder. It also has an impact on the brain regions in charge of your attention, memory, and decision-making.

Medication. The way that brain chemicals function can be altered by some medicines. Your concentration and memory may be affected. Among these are medicines for:
- Sleep
- Allergies
- Incontinence (when your bladder is uncontrollable)
- Depression
- Spasms of muscles

Thyroid issues. This gland produces hormones that are essential for many bodily processes, including thinking. You can find it difficult to focus if your thyroid gland produces either too little or too much.

Other Factors That May Influence Focus:
Your attention span may also suffer from the following:

Stress. According to experts, when you're anxious, the survival-related portion of your brain takes control. Your brain's other regions, such as those that govern attention and thought, receive less energy.

Hunger. To function, your brain requires energy. It's challenging to focus when your blood sugar levels drop.

Multitasking. It could appear time-saving to work on a report while responding to emails and taking conference calls. Yet, trying to do too much at once might backfire. Our brains are designed to focus on a single task at a time. According to research, switching gears frequently reduces efficiency and increases the likelihood of errors.

Inadequate sleep. When you're fatigued, it's difficult to focus. This is because while you sleep, your brain cells renew and rejuvenate. When you don't get enough sleep, they don't work as well. According to research, missing even one night of sleep makes it more difficult to focus and tune out distractions.

Eating a lot of fatty or sweet stuff. Sugar quickly raises blood sugar levels, which is followed by an energy drop. Although unhealthy saturated fat-rich diets may cause inflammation that harms your brain. According to one study, women performed worse on an attention test after consuming a meal high in unsaturated fat.

How to Recognize When Your Level of Attention Is Low

Everyone experiences occasional problems focusing. It's typical. You may be wondering why you can't focus at all and before you know it, you've skipped a meal.

When you find yourself unable to focus on a single task, it's important to consider the larger picture. While considering your capacity for focus, consider yourself as a Whole Person. You can find it difficult to complete crucial chores and make decisions in your personal life if you're having trouble clearing your mind. Moreover, less mental clarity makes it challenging to focus or see past life's stresses.

Some indicators of a lack of attention are simpler to spot than others. Observe the warning indicators listed below:

- You experience mental haze: You feel physically exhausted and cognitively disoriented when you have brain fog, and everything takes longer to absorb. Brain fog that lasts longer than six months may indicate chronic fatigue syndrome.
- You have trouble making simple decisions: How soon can you make a lunchtime decision? Your levels of attention may be poor if you feel like you have trouble thinking clearly or that your thoughts wander when you try to make decisions.
- You put off things a lot: Time management is a crucial yet challenging skill. Time can fly by so quickly, but if you have trouble managing your calendar, your attention levels may require improvement. To

improve your ability to focus and reduce procrastination, you may need to make some changes to your way of living.

- When you catch yourself daydreaming, it might be challenging to restore focus and complete your regular chores. If you can't stay present, tasks like mowing the grass, cleaning the dishes, or even watching an entire movie might become challenging.

Determine Your Distractions

When are you unable to focus on anything? Lack of focus can have many possible causes, but ultimately it is referred to as being distracted.

If you have difficulties focusing, you are the best person to figure out your distractions. Not everyone will notice that you haven't been getting enough sleep or that you are having personal difficulties. To comprehend what's occurring if you haven't identified your distractors, you'll need to improve your self-awareness.

Distractors might be of two different kinds:

Internal thoughts and anxieties, such as worrying about something humiliating you did or getting ready to deliver a speech, are examples of internal distractions.

Distractions from the outside, such as a noisy workplace, an unpleasant scent, or attractive things nearby, are factors outside your control.

Beware of Burnout

Burnout is a significant factor in attention loss. We all have hectic days at work, but if we overwork ourselves, we'll burn out. After being intensely focused on a task, our brains become worn out.

We, therefore, require a suitable work-life balance as well as downtime. Different types of sleep enable our bodies and minds to regenerate.

To improve our ability to concentrate, we must also make sure we are feeding ourselves. Our brain function and general mental health have been discovered to be significantly impacted by food. Our brain and behavior are influenced by our gut microbiome, which is made up of all the bacteria and germs in our digestive tract.

And when factors like bad sleep patterns or improper diets disturb our gut microbiota, it affects our mental health and brain growth. Green leafy vegetables and strawberries are two meals that have a favorable effect on brain health, however, excessive amounts of caffeine and sugar might have a detrimental effect on our ability to focus.

Burnout must be taken seriously, particularly at work. To prevent taking on too many initiatives, we should identify our roles and duties. To prevent working too much, it's crucial to have moral character and be open and honest with our bosses about our level of energy.

Chapter 3

The Focusing Power of Meditation

Meditation is a well-liked method for unwinding and relieving tension that may greatly improve your capacity for focus and attention. Focus is the capacity to give full attention to one subject while neglecting all others, which may be exceedingly challenging in a culture that values multitasking and achievement. Developing your attention can help you be more creative, improve your problem-solving abilities, and experience less stress while managing many tasks at once.

Firstly, Pay Attention to Your Breathing

According to Mayo Clinic, the goal of meditation is to focus on one subject while letting other ideas drift past. It can be intimidating for someone who has trouble focusing on just one thing, which includes most of us. Just paying attention to your breathing is a simple way to get started.

To avoid being distracted by physical discomfort, choose a comfortable seat. Next, shut your eyes and focus only on your breathing.

Do not attempt to regulate the depth or rate of your breaths; simply inhale and exhale through your nose.

Let your thoughts drift away while you focus on paying attention to your breath whenever they try to invade your meditation. Feel the passage of it through your throat. Feel your belly grow. As long as you can, stay here.

Secondly, Stay Still

Most individuals twitch easily. Although it's still a rather strange concept, sitting correctly can improve focus by putting you in charge of your physical body rather than allowing your comfort to dictate how you feel. Do not be concerned about hearing your breath, and try to sit as comfortably as you can. Try not to budge an eyelid or a muscle while you close your eyes. You'll experience constant itching, facial hair that prickles, and achy joints. Do not give in to anything until you are feeling the pain that is more severe than usual discomfort. Your mind will become calmer and your ability to focus will gradually improve as you practise the attention necessary to ignore your body and sit motionless.

Thirdly, Use Mantra

Try introducing a mantra after you feel at ease being motionless and can easily pay attention to your breathing for lengthy periods. A mantra is merely a word, syllable, or phrase that is repeated to aid in focus. Repeat your mantra repeatedly when you are in meditation.

The phrase "ohm," which you utter on each exhalation, is a straightforward example. You must focus to keep your mind motionless while you enter the sound since ideas will attempt to rush back into your head when you inhale. Your capacity to consistently focus on one item while being interrupted will improve as a result.

How to Use Meditation to Improve Focus?

Here are some strategies for utilizing meditation's ability to help you focus.

1. Determine why you wish to focus. You could frequently wish to focus to "get more done" or "be more productive."

2. Identify the distractions in your life. Daniel Goleman, the author of Attention, distinguishes between sensory and emotional distractions. He also warns readers that being distracted increases your risk of making errors, being mentally exhausted, and becoming stressed. A break from your thoughts, relief from the intense sensory experiences of an open workplace or a crowded home, and the sensation of serenity or quiet among the bustle of daily life are all made possible by focus meditation, which also slows down your body.

3. Envision the result. One of my favorite pictures is of the focus as light. Every one of us is illuminated to some extent. The

objective is to energetically transform yours from a diffuse light that lets you see the whole stage to a spotlight that shines on one specific item while leaving everything else in the dark.

4. Ask your mind where it goes when it is preoccupied. Where does your mind wander when you find yourself losing focus? Dreaming, reliving the past, or making plans for the future? When practicing focus meditation, you repeatedly bring your awareness back to your breath or a mantra. This is similar to doing brain curls. It improves your capacity to recognize when you are focusing on something other than what you intended to do and to redirect your attention to what you intended.

5. Set timers for 20 minutes on chores. Every morning, make a list of your to-dos and devote 20 minutes to each item on the list. Add the assignment back at the end if you don't complete what has to be done in the specified time. Take a little break to

stretch, walk, or go outside every 20 minutes. Every one of us has the same number of 24-hour days.

Your ability to multitask is continually tested, yet it is less efficient than focusing on a single activity. Use the power of meditation to sharpen your attention and enhance your focus by using these mindfulness meditation strategies.

Chapter 4

Reclaiming Your Focus

Imagine yourself drafting an email when your phone suddenly beeps with a text message alert. You descend to read the message and perhaps even respond. You return to checking your email after a little delay. Now that you've gotten off track, you have to go back and read what you've previously written to finish your point.

Switching cost refers to the time it takes to return to the work at hand after being interrupted. The mental expense we incur when we switch our focus from one item to another and back again is known as the switching cost.

Thankfully, improving one's ability to focus can lower switching costs and increase productivity.

In today's social media-dominated digital environment, maintaining attention may seem practically impossible, but there is good news.

You can recover your attention—and your life—by learning how to focus successfully with the right information and a few sound techniques.

Focused attention is the capacity to concentrate on one object at a time. Our brains are always looking for informational stimuli. They are operating at full capacity. Our brains just can't digest all of the information that is in front of us because there is simply too much of it. As we may choose what to focus on from the facts at hand, it is up to our "attention" to do so.

Both in our personal and professional lives, the focus is essential for success. At work, being able to focus on one task at a time might make the difference between doing your job successfully or poorly. You may achieve superior outcomes, enhance time management, and give your team and clients your undivided attention by concentrating. The success of a corporation depends on its ability to pay close attention to detail. Clients, team members, and leaders all want to know that you are attentive and listening.

If they do, they'll also participate and pay attention, which will raise the organization's morale and productivity overall.

Ten Strategies for Increasing Attention and Reclaiming Focus

Focus improvement requires time and repetition. Hence, while better focus won't happen immediately, these 10 techniques will help you focus more intently over time.

1. Water Intake

To be hydrated, our bodies require between 11 and 15 glasses of water daily. It comes to 3.7 liters. Any less than that can lead to dehydration, which impairs attention and other cognitive abilities. According to the National Library of Medicine, dehydration can have a particularly detrimental effect on brain function in youngsters and the elderly. By establishing a daily fluid goal, carrying a water bottle, being aware of how frequently to refill it, and setting reminders, you can ensure that your mind and body remain hydrated throughout the day.

2. Meditation and Mindfulness Exercises

Mind wandering is one of the main distractions from attention. This might happen while we're focusing on a job and then suddenly remember a discussion we had the day before or what we want to eat. All of us engage in it. Thankfully, as Dr. Amishi Jha explains, mind wandering may be controlled by engaging in mindfulness exercises. She emphasizes in her TEDx talk that mindfulness is paying attention to the current moment with awareness. And without reacting emotionally to what is occurring in any way.

The advantages will increase if you practice mindfulness more frequently. According to studies, even only 10–12 minutes of meditation five days a week can significantly increase one's capacity for sustained focus.

3. Journaling

Writing down your ideas might help you focus and concentrate much better if you set out time each day to do it. Writing down your thoughts might help you figure out what's causing your worry, anxiety, or distraction. Finding the root of the problem will enable you to come up with remedies and feel more at peace. Journaling has been demonstrated to lessen sadness, control anxiety, and increase attention when paired with other healthy lifestyle practices.

4. Regular Workout

Exercising for at least 30 minutes each day can significantly improve cognitive performance. We increase blood flow to the brain when we start moving our body and even start to perspire. Our entire body's overall health depends on proper circulation. According to the World Health Organization, persons between the ages of 18 and 64 should engage in at least 150 to 300 minutes of vigorous aerobic exercise each week to reap the health advantages, including enhanced cognitive function.

5. Eating Well

How we feel and think can be impacted by what we eat. Our bodies and brains may not be receiving the vitamins and supplements they require to function at their peak if we aren't getting enough of certain critical elements from our meals. "Eat your colors" and make sure each meal has a range of nutrients to increase attention. The health and clarity of the brain are directly connected to several meals, including berries, fatty fish, and green vegetables.

6. Maintaining Healthy Sleep Hygiene

Good sleep hygiene is crucial for our health and many other aspects of our life. Our brain cells renew and rejuvenate when we sleep. We go through this procedure to feel relaxed and invigorated the next day. Make your bedroom relaxing and sleep-inducing, avoid stimulation an hour before bed and practice good sleep hygiene by avoiding coffee, alcohol, and sweets.

7. Taking Breaks

Giving our thoughts a break by taking a break is like doing the same. When we focus on anything for a prolonged amount of time—like preparing for a test, for instance—our minds are likely to start to wander because they are worn out. It's important to take a break at this time. Your mind can have a chance to rest by doing anything as simple as taking a little stroll, listening to music, or making a phone call to a friend. When you come back to the activity, your mind will be renewed and able to focus.

8. Make Smart Goals

When we have a lot to accomplish, it might be easy to lose concentration and direction if we don't have a clear strategy. For instance, coming back to work after a lengthy vacation can include confronting a huge list of unopened emails, important assignments, and conference calls. Or perhaps your firm is scaling. The beginning might be intimidating. Thankfully, by defining and creating **S.M.A.R.T.** objectives—that is, goals that are Specific, Measurable, Achievable, Relevant, and Time-Bound—you may restore focus, clarity, and direction.

To set a **S.M.A.R.T.** goal, adhere to this standard:

Specific: What has to be done, specifically? What specific actions must be taken to complete it?

Measurable: How will the goal's success be determined?

Achievable: Is the objective reachable? Can it be done?

Relevant: Do other priorities and the goal's priority line up?

Time-Bound: When will the objective be accomplished?

9. Take in Some Music

You won't have any problem locating music playlists designed expressly for focus if you have an Apple Music, Spotify, or Youtube account. Many playlists are likely to appear when you put "focus music" or "study music" into the search box. This is because appropriate music not only serves as a fantastic therapeutic aid in general but may also promote attention. Try listening to relaxing background or classical music the next time you need to focus. Instead of distracting cheerful music with lyrics, listening to relaxing music may help you focus.

10.Get Rid of All Internal and External Distractions

We may drastically improve our capacity to maintain focused attention by limiting our exposure to and sensitivity to internal and external distractions. It's crucial to develop habits or modify your routine to guarantee that there are as few distractions as possible when you need to focus. Perhaps this entails setting up specified times of the day when you won't plan any calls or keep your phone quiet. Even a little period of looking through social media may be internally distracting and send our minds into digressions. Be sure to cut out as many distractions as you can to keep your attention focused on the present.

Your Mental Health May Be Improved with Daily Mindfulness

While we are imprisoned by the delusion of multitasking, our minds cannot be liberated into the present moment.

It's a prevalent misconception that multitasking increases efficiency. But, research demonstrates that our brains are unable to manage and interpret several impulses at once. So even if we think we're "multitasking," we're not paying attention to several things at once. We are just moving from one item to another rapidly while losing efficiency in the process.

Developing awareness is the secret to mastering focus. It's an atomic habit that will keep you in the here and now and provide you clarity over what to focus on. It could be beneficial to consider your main primary goal when engaging in mindfulness exercises. What is the major goal you have in mind? You may refocus your attention and reorder your priorities by engaging in visualization exercises. Your productivity will increase, and your general mental health will also benefit.

Chapter 5

Seeking Help

It's not a big deal if you forget to flip over your laundry because you can't focus. Yet, it's time to obtain medical help if you neglect to eat or if your physical and mental health deteriorates.

Discussing your lack of focus with your doctor, a psychologist, or another medical expert will help you discover solutions. Your ability to focus may be affected by several diseases, and your doctor can develop a treatment plan to assist you to do so.

You could find that using prescription drugs like Adderall or Ritalin helps you focus, but you should first consult a healthcare provider.

If your inability to concentrate is significantly disrupting your life, speak with your doctor. You could observe, for instance, that you're lagging in your work or studies.

Also schedule a consultation if any of these symptoms are observed:

- Persistent dejection, despair, or remorse
- Alterations to your sleeping patterns, such as difficulty falling asleep or excessive sleep
- Months-long worry and anxiety that interferes with your daily existence
- Fatigued without cause
- Constipation, swollen face, raspy voice, and/or dry skin
- Heat intolerance, unintentional weight loss, and sleeplessness

The following six indications should prompt you to seek emergency medical attention:

1. Sudden forgetfulness, such as forgetting your name or where you are
2. Severe migraines that make you feel ill
3. Sleep deficit or absence of sleep

4. Longer than six-month-long brain fog that weakens your cognitive abilities
5. Confusion between losing consciousness and waking up
6. Your performance at work or in school is less effective than normal.

Everyone goes through a distinct journey when trying to overcome a lack of attention. Not all tactics and advice work for everyone. Try new approaches over and over until you find one that works for you. To stop bothersome alerts, try using the Pomodoro technique, keeping a notebook, or turning off your phones. The important thing is to persevere. This is crucial: your efforts won't go in vain.

Improve your attention by making the following adjustments to bolster your concentration:

Time frame. Have a ton of responsibilities? Set aside precise times to do each work, such as a half-hour each in the morning and the afternoon for email checking and phone answering. This prevents you from juggling many tasks at once.

Regularly moving about. You may unwind, get better sleep, and reduce tension with its assistance. Moreover, it reduces inflammation and promotes the production of new brain cells. In the long term, that could help you think more clearly.

Eat sensibly. To stave off hunger and maintain a stable blood sugar level, eat meals high in fiber, unsaturated fat, and lean protein in addition to fruits and vegetables. They provide the vitamins B, C, E, and magnesium that your brain needs to function.

Eliminate distractions. When you need to concentrate, try to choose a peaceful spot. Take away anything that frequently vying for your attention. You might wish to mute the radio or TV and disable your phone's alerts for a while.